The Man with Small Hands

Jed Harris

Copyright © 2017 Jed Harris

All rights reserved.

ISBN: **0692967338**
ISBN-13: **978-0692967331**

This book is dedicated to all of those who stand up to bullies.

The only time he felt good, was when he used Twitter to send a falsehood.

He began to spread lies Tweet after Tweet,
And soon he discovered that his fingers began to retreat.

He could not even hold a toothbrush, His breath began to smell and his face would blush.

**But soon he learned,
that if he stopped sending mean Tweets
his hands returned.**

If he started to help people instead of telling lies, his hands grew back to their normal size.

Soon he decided to resign,
And be a hand model for Kalvin Klein.

www.ingramcontent.com/pod-product-compliance
Lightning Source LLC
Chambersburg PA
CBHW041814040426
42450CB00004B/157